THE MANAGER'S POCKET GUIDE TO

Training

Shawn Doyle

HRD PRESS, INC.
Amherst, Massachusetts

Copyright © 2006, HRD Press, Inc.

All rights reserved. No part of this publication may be reproduced or transmitted in any form or by any means, electronic or mechanical, including photocopy, recording, or used in an information storage or retrieval system, without prior written permission from the author.

Published by: HRD Press, Inc.
                22 Amherst Road
                1-800-822-2801
                (U.S. and Canada)
                1-413-253-3488
                1-413-253-3490 (Fax)
                www.hrdpress.com

ISBN 0-87425-925-8

Cover design by Eileen Klockars
Production services by Anctil Virtual Office
Editorial services by Suzanne Bay and Sally Farnham

Dedication

This book is dedicated to Cindy Doyle my wife, advisor, and best friend. Thanks for believing in me all these years—your support has always meant so much. You are amazing.

Table of Contents

Foreword vii
Chapter One: Why Train? 1
   Benefits of Training to the Organization 2
   The Benefits of Training for Customers
      when Employees are Trained 5
   Why it is Important for Leaders to Understand Training 6

Chapter Two: Defining and Leveraging Training 13
   What is training? 14
   When is training needed? 20

Chapter Three: How People Learn 29
   How do people learn? 29
   Learning Styles 33
   Accelerated Learning 36
   Positioning Your Training as a "Win" 40
   Timing is everything! 44
   The Importance of Fun in Training 47

Chapter Four: Types of Training 49
   Classroom Training 49
   E-learning 51
   Self-Study 53
   Outside Seminars 55
   Videos and DVDs 57
   Audio CDs 59

Chapter Five: Sources for Training Delivery 61
   The Human Resources Department 61
   Training Department or Corporate University 62
   Outside Consultants 63
   Training Vendors 63
   "Red Flags" 64

Chapter Six: Working with the Team 69
The Growth and Development Meeting 72

Chapter Seven: Looking at the Future 77
Return on Investment... 77
Managing the Training Function 78
Keeping up with the Training Industry................................. 79

Foreword

I travel the country facilitating training programs on leadership, sales, motivation, and communications. Often, at the end of a session, I have people come over to me, shake my hand, and say something like: "I honestly didn't want to be here because I've had training before, but this was really great. I'm glad I came." When I read the written responses on the training evaluation forms, they all have a similar theme:

"Wow! This was really—I mean *really*—good!"
"I wasn't expecting much . . . thanks."
"Much more than I thought I would get! Thank you."
"I was prepared not to like today, but I did!"
"Training is usually dry and boring, but this wasn't."
"Better than the training we usually have."

The insinuation woven into both the written and the verbal comments is simple. Training is usually poorly facilitated, bone dry, and about as entertaining as watching paint dry. So who do we blame for training's sad state of affairs? Well, its very simple—leaders. I know that this is an outrageous statement to make. Why not blame the trainers, Human Resources, or the hotel where the meeting was held? How about the surly, unruly participants? Aren't *they* responsible for embracing the training? No. It is the *leader's* obligation and responsibility. It is the leader's fault for setting up, sponsoring (either explicitly or implicitly), endorsing, and paying for lousy training. As a leader, you get exactly what you will accept. One can make some safe assumptions about this situation:

1. Leaders don't have the tools and knowledge to know how to evaluate training.
2. Leaders don't have high standards for training.

3. Leaders don't make the time to carefully review the qualifications of those who are providing the training.
4. Leaders don't have a concrete idea as to what the real needs are of the ones who will be receiving the training.
5. Leaders don't know how to find the right resources to fill their needs.
6. Leaders are generalists, but training/development is a specialty.
7. Leaders don't make training a priority when they're trying to manage a thousand other projects, deadlines, and processes.
8. There is no long-term plan in place for training.

I have worked with many leaders in my career, leaders who have led teams to amazing levels of productivity and effectiveness. Those teams had undying loyalty and admiration for the person leading them. Outstanding leaders possess a passionate, dedicated commitment to training and development. They know that people want to learn and grow and that when they do, they are motivated and productive.

I've also seen the exact opposite—leaders who thought that training was silly, unnecessary, or redundant. "Why should I train anyone?" they'd ask. "I hired them for the skills that they already have. Why do they need training?" One look at their team tells you all that you need to know. The employees are stagnant, bored, and complacent.

Many leaders have never made the connection between training and results. They don't understand that training can truly drive performance to higher levels. Every year Fortune Magazine publishes a list of the "100 Best Companies to Work For." Each company is listed along with statistics. Among those statistics are the annual hours spent on training per employee. Here are 5 of the top 20 companies from 2006 along with their statistics on training:

Foreword

- #1—Genentech: 51 Hours
- #3—Valero Energy: 67 Hours
- #6—Container Store: 108 Hours
- #8—J. M. Smucker: 90 Hours
- #11—Boston Consulting Group: 106 Hours

The list of 100 is filled with examples of companies that invest between 40–106 hours per employee annually. Think about this: In some companies, they are investing 2½ weeks per year in development of each employee's skills and knowledge. Are we suggesting that every company should do this? Yes. No. Maybe. Obviously, there is something that these companies' leaders understand—that training leads to results. As a leader, you have to decide what is right for your team and organization.

Leaders must know how to leverage training resources both internally and externally in order to maximize performance. Do they have to be experts? No, just educated generalists. If leaders can learn enough to make reasoned, intelligent decisions about training activities and expenditures, then they can have training that is fun, exciting, relevant, and drives both enhanced performance and effectiveness. This book will teach you what to consider, what questions to ask, and where to find the resources that you need. Sound like a pipe dream? It's not. This book is the answer to all of the relevant questions that leaders have about training in a way that is short, simple, to the point, and digestible.

I sincerely hope that this book has an impact on how you look at training.

Chapter One
Why Train?

Training. Development. Coaching. Mentoring. Learning. Self-learning. Self-study. Education. Roundtables. Breakouts. Classes. We have all heard and used these terms in our leadership work. Some leaders find them a little confusing and are not really sure *what* they are and *why* they are important.

I have been involved in training and development for the past 19 years, 17 of which were spent in various corporate training roles. I have worked in and around Training departments, helped launch a corporate university, and run my own training and development company. In addition, I have written, designed, and developed over 100 original training programs. This broad and varied experience has given me a chance to observe leadership at all levels, in all kinds of organizations. The best leaders I have worked with have had a great understanding of training, a commitment to training their teams to meet the objectives of their department or organization, an ability to leverage both *inside and outside* resources for training, and a belief that training gives them a competitive edge.

As a leader, you are judged on the performance of your organization. Most of us know that performance means one thing and one thing only—*results.* As Donna Harrison, Senior Research Executive at MORI Human Resources Company once said, "Great leaders are never satisfied with the current levels of performance. They are restlessly driven by possibilities and potential achievements." The only thing that counts in most organizations is performance. If done the right way, training will be a major contributing factor to getting results. The purpose of this book is to help you understand *everything* that you need to know as a leader about training (even what you *don't need* to know), and to show you how to leverage training to get results.

Training will soon become the major competitive edge that leaders use to drive their organizations forward. The new generations of workers will not be part of the "gold watch" crowd (and probably won't even know what that is!). They won't be hanging around your organization or anybody else's long enough to collect a pension. Generations X and Y will work for organizations to learn new skills, and will then move on, taking those new skills to the next company. Since it's unlikely that these bright new stars will stay at your company until retirement, you goal, then, should be to keep them as employees as long as possible. To do this, you will have to give them new skills and developmental opportunities. Training is an essential part of that equation.

Benefits of Training to the Organization

A robust and well-thought-out training program benefits an organization as a whole in many ways.

Training increases retention. Having a sound training program in place is a great retention tool. Employees who are being trained and developed are much less likely to leave than those who are not. During a leadership-development course I was running for a client company, one of the participants said to me, "I just feel so special being part of this program. It makes me feel appreciated." Don't underestimate the importance of retention: If employees stay longer, they become more productive as they gain more experience, and this saves the company money because it doesn't have to pay recruitment and training costs of hiring a new employee. (These costs can be as much as 2 to 3 times an employee's annual salary!)

Chapter One: Why Train?

Training improves morale. Training leads to enhanced morale if it is done well and correctly. It also boosts self-esteem and confidence. As Wal-Mart founder Sam Walton once said, "Outstanding leaders go out of the way to boost the self-esteem of their personnel. If people believe in themselves, it's amazing what they can accomplish." I have worked with hundreds of people (maybe even thousands), and I have seen first-hand the transformational power (both as a facilitator and student) of training.

Training drives productivity. Productivity is greatly enhanced with training. If you are taking your luxury car to the shop for repairs, don't you want someone who is well trained doing the work? If you are having brain surgery, wouldn't you want it done by someone who is well trained? I am amazed at the number of times I am in a restaurant or in a store or on the phone and the person I am dealing with says, "Uhh . . . I don't know how to do that—let me check with my manager." Training helps employees understand the how, what, where, when, and why of their job. When they have that, they can work faster and with more efficiency.

Training saves money. It has been estimated that in the United States alone, errors cost millions every year. If that is the case, then literally thousands of dollars might be saved in your organization if people are trained well. Many managers say, "Well, that training is kind of expensive. I don't know if we should spend that kind of money on training." Many client companies I have worked with can't afford *not* to spend money on training, yet they have a hard time identifying the return on investment should they institute the training (more on that later).

Training builds a sense of "team." We are all so busy and so stretched today in corporate America. Every one is in a big hurry, traveling and working and going in all different directions. Often teams don't feel like teams at all, but rather a disparate group of individuals who simply work in the same department. Training delivers knowledge and skills, but also helps create that feeling of "team" through the sharing of a common experience.

Training builds "bench strength." I talk to many clients who have not addressed the issue of succession planning and making sure that the right people are in place should someone leave the organization. Training can help you build bench strength so that when positions need to be filled, they can be filled from within.

Training makes hiring easier. Let's think this one through. You are talking to two different companies about possibly working for them. One company tells you that it is committed to employee development, and that you will have training to help you grow and develop. At the next company, no one mentions training at all, and when you ask about it, they stutter and say, "Well, we can pay for outside training if you want to go to that kind of thing." So here is the big question: Which answer is more impressive? The answer is obvious. I have worked for companies where some departments did training and others didn't. The word traveled fast; most people wanted to work for the department that provided them training. Training is an effective way to attract superior candidates and make your company or department the "employer of choice." An individual who wants to grow and develop is the kind of employee every leader wants.

Training saves time. When employees are well trained, it saves time because there is less confusion and less redundancy. If an employee knows how to do their job and has had the training, then they are much less likely to have to ask for direction and support from the manager. They will have an increased level of self-sufficiency.

Training increases confidence. George Herbert, 17th century English poet, once said, "Skill and confidence are an unconquered army." When employees get training that they need and their skills improve, their performance is enhanced. This leads to employees who have a high level of confidence because they

Chapter One: Why Train?

know they are competent. I once sat in the lobby of a large chain hotel waiting for my ride to the airport when I found myself staring at the desk clerk. This young man, who was no more than 22 years old, performed his tasks not just well, but *brilliantly*. I watched him handle each guest with enthusiasm, knowledge, competence, and confidence. He radiated a positive attitude. It was clear to me that part of the reason was simple—*he knew what he was doing.*

Trained employees represent the company well. Each time an employee interacts with a customer, a vendor, or a supplier, he or she is representing the company. To the customer, the employee *is* the company; they become the face of the company. The better the training, the better they represent the company in a positive light.

The Benefits of Training for Customers when Employees are Trained

In addition to the organization benefiting from employee training, customers gain advantages from doing business with well-trained employees.

The customer gets better service. Customers get better, more-efficient service when they are being helped by a well-trained employee. I once ordered something at a deli and found out after the fact that they didn't take credit cards. When I voiced some displeasure with this policy, the reply was, "We don't take credit cards because it slows us down." If the employee had been trained in how to handle these kinds of complaints, it probably wouldn't have bothered me, but the answer was all about *them* and not about pleasing the *customer*.

The customer saves time. When I go into a business and the employee helps me find what I need and I can get out of there quickly, I am very happy with my experience. The same thing applies on the phone: I don't want to spend my valuable time waiting while an employee fumbles around looking for the answer. I recently received a refund from my home state of Pennsylvania that had been delayed for more than six months. Every time I called to check on it, I talked to someone who was able to look up my record efficiently and tell me what was going on up to that moment.

The customer feels good about their experience. Customers who come in contact with well-trained employees leave the business (literally or virtually) feeling good about the experience. Because they feel good about the experience, they come back and tell their friends about the organization.

Why it is Important for Leaders to Understand Training

As a leader, it is essential that you know about training and how it can be used to drive the results of your department, your team, or your organization. Admittedly, we live in an age where leaders must be generalists; it's impossible to be skilled in all areas and an expert on everything. The idea is to know enough to get the training to serve your own specific goals and objectives. Just like computers or software or data or reports, training is a tool to help achieve your objectives.

There are 10 reasons why it is *specifically useful* to have a better understanding of training:

1. When you evaluate a training program or product, you will know what to look for.
2. You will know what questions to ask to make important decisions about training.
3. You will have a good idea about who should be involved in the decision-making process.

Chapter One: Why Train?

4. You will save money by making wise decisions about spending training dollars.
5. You will know how to find the resources you need to get the job done.
6. If you do the training yourself, you will know how to find the right resources.
7. If you hire an outside resource, you will know what to look for.
8. You will know how to negotiate for competitive pricing because you will know where the market is in terms of current pricing.
9. You will be able to create a reasonable budget for training that is based on reality.
10. You will feel more confident and competent in the world of training.

Before we go any further, it would be helpful to get an idea as to where you are in the spectrum of training. (Please do not skip this step—I know how leaders are!)

A short self-assessment appears on the next page. Take time to read each of the questions. Respond to the best of your ability, using a scale of 1 to 10 (1 = strongly disagree; 10 = strongly agree). Circle the number that best represents your response.

The Manager's Pocket Guide to Training

Training Analysis

	Strongly Disagree ⟵ ⟶ Strongly Agree										Total
I am very knowledgeable about training.	1	2	3	4	5	6	7	8	9	10	
I like training and think it has great value.	1	2	3	4	5	6	7	8	9	10	
I have had a great deal of training.	1	2	3	4	5	6	7	8	9	10	
I have done a lot of training as a facilitator.	1	2	3	4	5	6	7	8	9	10	
I am a continuous learner.	1	2	3	4	5	6	7	8	9	10	
I think training is important for my team.	1	2	3	4	5	6	7	8	9	10	
Everyone should participate in training.	1	2	3	4	5	6	7	8	9	10	
I am aware of my internal resources in my organization.	1	2	3	4	5	6	7	8	9	10	
I am aware of my external resources.	1	2	3	4	5	6	7	8	9	10	
I understand how people learn.	1	2	3	4	5	6	7	8	9	10	
Grand total score:											

(Scoring directions are on the next page.)

Chapter One: Why Train?

Scoring Directions for Training Analysis Self-Assessment

Write the answer for each horizontal row in the Total column (the far right column). Now add up the numbers in the Total column and record the final number in the bottom right corner.

The perfect grand total score is 100. Here is how to look at your score:

- **100–90** Congratulations! This book should just be a tune-up for you.
- **89–80** You are pretty knowledgeable about training.
- **79–70** We are glad to have you with us. Welcome!
- **70–0** It's why you bought the book in the first place!

♦ ♦ ♦ ♦ ♦ ♦ ♦ ♦

Now that a general understanding has been reached as to where you are on the spectrum, here is what you can expect from the rest of this book, which is full of tools, techniques, and ideas to help you become more conversant and effective in training:

Chapter Two: Defining and Leveraging Training. This chapter explores how you leverage training to your advantage. You will be given a useful definition of training and learn how to determine when training is needed and when it is not needed. In addition, we'll present 10 key things every leader should know about training, as well as some of the myths about training.

Chapter Three: How People Learn. Leaders must know some of the basic elements of training (how people learn, the importance of behavioral styles, accelerated learning, how to set up the *right kind* of training environment, etc.). We'll discuss key factors in training in general. Training should also be fun; we will make some suggestions on ways to make training fun (and more importantly, explain why fun is important).

Chapter Four: Types of Training. There are many different kinds of training. If training is your entire tool kit, then training methods are the tools. This chapter will provide an in-depth look at the different methods that can be used to train your team. This will broaden the possibilities and provide important variety in your approach.

Chapter Five: Sources for Training Delivery. Once you know the types of training that are possible, you must determine where to find the resources that you will need to set up the program. In this section, you will learn about some great "hidden" resources. A big part of knowledge is simply knowing where to look.

Chapter Six: Working with the Team. You now have a basic understanding about training and resources. You're ready to go full steam ahead, right? Wrong. How can a leader move forward if he or she has not identified what is really needed? This is like a doctor writing a prescription before making a diagnosis! Bad. Very bad. This section will provide tools and techniques for quickly making a determination as to what is needed and who needs it.

Chapter Seven: Looking at the Future. Once your short-term plans are in place, it is time to take a longer-term view. What kind of ROI do you want from the training? What type of budget do you need to set up? How do you "bottom line" all of this for the people to whom you report on a consistent basis? In this section, you'll find all of the tools and techniques to head in that direction.

Training just makes sense in this competitive world. Remember that employees have choices: to work with you, or not; to work for your company, or not; to work to their full potential, or not. A leader who is committed to training takes the team to new levels of performance.

Chapter One: Why Train?

As motivational speaker Jim Rohn once said, "A good objective of leadership is to help those who are doing poorly to do well and to help those who are doing well to do even better." I can't think of a better way to do that than through training.

Chapter Two
Defining and Leveraging Training

The first question any leader might logically ask is this: *"What is training?"* Yes, I know most of us have experienced training, but was it training or education? Is there really a difference? And if there is, why does it matter?

Let's start with a simple exercise to help define training more clearly. In the box below is a list of 20 activities. Place a checkmark in the Training column if you consider the activity to be training.

Activity	Training?
Attending a class in the company	
E-learning	
Reading a book	
Being coached by an executive	
Job shadowing	
Studying a manual	
Having a mentor	
Watching a video	
Listening to an audio CD	
Attending a meeting	
Attending industry conferences	
Participating in teleseminars	
Reading an e book	
Meeting with your boss	
Working on a special project	
Doing research	
Visiting other locations	
Working with other employees	
Conducting an employee meeting	
Participating in a Toastmasters group	

So, how many activities do you consider to be training? Depending on the circumstance, each one can be considered training. That doesn't mean that they always are, but they are all training opportunities.

Leaders do not always appreciate the variety of forms training can take. This is one thing we want you to think about as you read this book. Training isn't just classroom learning or e-learning—many forms and combinations are possible. The key is to have the right prescription written for the right diagnosis. As a leader, you have to know how to leverage training to your advantage. The first step is to get a clear definition of training.

What is training?

Merriam-Webster's Collegiate Dictionary defines training as "to form by instruction, discipline, or drill: to teach so as to make fit, qualified, or proficient." Training, in a nutshell, is about developing skills, improving performance, increasing knowledge, and most importantly improving performance. As Queen Elizabeth once said, "It's all to do with the training; you can do a lot if you are properly trained." Professional athletes have trainers for nutrition, workout scheduling, and so on. Why shouldn't your employees increase their performance as well, through training?

So now that we have a clear idea of what training is, let's take a look at some of the myths about training that training professionals have run into time and again. I don't know how these myths started or where they come from, but they seem to be prevalent in all of my experience.

Chapter Two: Defining and Leveraging Training

Myth #1: Training is not necessary.

I once met with the owner of a company that had been in business for a very long time. The owner was in his sixties and was very set in his ways. When I asked him about the kind of training he was providing for his employees, he looked at me and said, "Why do they need training? They already know how to do their job." I explained that employees need ongoing training to keep up with the latest skills so that they can be prepared for future opportunities. He wasn't buying that concept at all. In his mind, business was good and cash was flowing in—so why train? My argument is that if business is good, it might be *great* if employees all perform at the highest levels. "Spend lavishly on training," says Tom Peters, career and business coach. "You can't spend too much on training." So the question a leader should ask is not "Should we do training?" but rather "How much training should we do, and how can we get the best results?"

Myth #2: Training is an event.

I once received a panicked call from a manager who was concerned about several issues. The conversation went something like this: "I need some help. I have a team that is spread out all over the country, and they are not feeling like or acting like a team. It is more like a bunch of separate teams." After I thought about the in-depth description he gave me, I asked him a question: "How much time do you have for a meeting?" He said he could give me the entire day. (So far so good.) I asked him what his expectations were—what he wanted to get out of the day. "At the end of that day, I want them to feel like a team." I told him that this would not happen—we could start the process, but it would take several steps and many months, if not a few years, to make that a reality. The problem will not be solved with one day or one week or one month of training. Write this down on your forehead if you need to.

> Training must be a process that involves follow-up and follow-through for the long term.

Otherwise, the cookies were nice, but nothing will be achieved.

Myth #3: Anyone can facilitate training.

This thinking is as absurd as someone saying that anyone can do brain surgery or fly a plane or paint a portrait. Facilitating training is an activity that involves skills, knowledge, talent, and experience. All of us have attended a training class at one time or another that was conducted by a front-line person who thought he or she could do it effectively, yet it ended up being a disaster. I have been conducting professional training for 19 years at the writing of this book, and have experienced *every* training disaster situation possible. I have gained a ton of knowledge about how to handle these situations and how to make the training experience as effective as possible for the learners. A front-line person, on the other hand, might have product or company knowledge, but no knowledge about adult learning theory, learning styles, group dynamics, or how to handle difficult participants. If you use inside resources, choose carefully and make sure the individual is trained in how to do training effectively. Keep this in mind: The results of the training will be in direct correlation to the skill of the trainer.

Myth #4: Training is only needed when someone is in a new role or assumes a new responsibility.

So not true! All employees should have an individual development plan. Great leaders know that the way to grow the company and grow the team is to have a constant and focused strategy to get everyone on the team growing and developing their skills—managers and supervisors and every single person on the team. Some leaders say, "Well, you want me to give training to the lowest level of employees in our company?" Yes, yes, and yes! The reasons are very simple: (1) They deserve it. (2) Performance will increase and morale will be high. Business guru Peter Drucker said, "Leadership is not magnetic personality—that can just as well be a glib tongue. It is not making friends and influencing people—that is flattery. Leadership is lifting a person's performance to a higher standard, the building of personality beyond its normal limits."

Chapter Two: Defining and Leveraging Training

Myth #5: Training can't be fun or funny or entertaining.

Some leaders with whom I have worked seem to think that training that is fun or funny or entertaining is not relevant or effective—to them, training has to be serious, boring, and deadly. That is not realistic: Training must be somewhat entertaining, or the individual will shut down and not learn at all. We live in a society of high content, high energy, and high entertainment; even the news broadcasts are now a high-energy mix of news and entertainment. If you ask someone to sit in a classroom and be lectured to for eight hours, imagine the result.

Trainers must use solid tools and techniques that are highly interactive and entertaining. There is a scientific reason for this: In the late 1960s, Bulgarian professor of psychiatry and psychotherapy, Georgi Lozanov conducted research studies on how people learn. The field of accelerated learning emerged from this research. Accelerated learning is based on the premise that people learn better when they are involved and as many senses are being called on as possible. So the senses of taste, smell, touch, and visual and auditory senses are all essential; they make the training much more effective, and increase learning and retention dramatically. So it is not fun just for fun's sake—it is fun *because it works.*

Myth #6: Training is formal, and it is done in a classroom.

Training in a classroom is only one form of training. There are many other forms and delivery methods that are often better and more cost-effective, and might have more impact. When you think of training, think of it as more than just a classroom. (We will explore this subject in more detail later in the book.)

Myth #7: You can cut the time for training and still have it work.

Many leaders I've worked with as an employee or as a consultant have asked the magic question, "I know the training class is eight hours, but can you cut it down to two?" They seem to always want the *Readers' Digest* condensed version. They hint that maybe getting rid of all of the exercises can reduce the program down to its core essence, but true professionals know that learning takes time and that the exercises are where learners apply the concepts and where the real learning occurs. To me, that is the difference between training and education: Education is when you learn about something, while training is when you learn how to *apply* information and use it in real-life work situations. So don't ask your internal and external trainers to cut training time. There is a specific reason why it is the length that it is.

Myth #8: Training has to be expensive.

No, training doesn't have to be expensive, especially if it is being done internally. If you have an on-staff trainer or the training is being conducted by an internal front-line person, then it can be done very inexpensively. The in-house person can design and facilitate the programs. There are many other effective external options available to you that are not that expensive. I once trained one of my staff members in a very significant area for a grand total of $22 (the cost of two books). Each week, we would read a chapter and then get together and discuss it. Voila! Problem solved. Training can be done inexpensively. If you *don't do it,* however, it's going to be really expensive! I once worked for a sign company that hand-fabricated an aluminum sign that was over 60 feet long and 4 feet wide. I went to check on the oversized sign (which I had sold) and noticed that it had been painted the wrong color. *The wrong color!* How much did it cost to fix? I assure you—a ton in both labor and materials. The company didn't believe in or provide training of any sort. If the company had implemented a training program in quality assurance, I think the mistake would never have happened.

Chapter Two: Defining and Leveraging Training

Myth #9: If we have e-learning, it will replace the classroom training.

I have seen so many articles in trade journals and other media that read something like this: "Magamega Corporation announces a major e-leaning initiative that will save the company $15 million in training costs." This is followed by the statement from the CEO in which the implied message is *Boy, aren't we smart. Can you believe how much we saved and how much our stock is going to go up, and how much more our employees love us now?* It is utter nonsense. Is e-learning effective? It can be at times. Can e-learning be a complete replacement for live one-on-one or group training? There ain't no way and ain't no how. Let me tell you why. It is very simple: E-learning can be very good for education and for pre-assignments, but it can't replace the classroom because in the classroom, learning takes place through or during exercises, discussions, and dialogue.

Myth #10: Executives don't do training.

Many organizational leaders say, "If we have a class, our executives won't attend as participants." The suggestion is that executives will be afraid to show that they don't know something, or their egos are so big that they aren't able to admit to themselves and others they need development. Since no one is perfect and everyone needs development, this argument doesn't hold water. Here's the key to getting executives to attend training: It must come as a request from the CEO, and the programs must be positioned as executive or leadership development. Both of these approaches can help get around the problem of "egotis giantitus."

Those are the most prevalent myths about training that I've seen. I am sure there are some I haven't heard of or some that will bubble to the surface as the corporate world continues to change. Your job is to avoid making those same assumptions and get around the myths. Focus on the real world: results.

When is training needed?

How does a leader know when training is needed? Be aware. Observe and process as much as you can so that you will recognize a problem and be able to make training part of the solution.

Here are some situations where training is absolutely essential:

When a new employee is hired. When a new employee is hired, he or she should always get new-employee orientation. Many organizations have no such thing. If your company doesn't, it doesn't mean that your team can't have one! Get the team together and create one. Great leaders are proactive: They don't wait until something is available.

Every employee who starts on your team must receive employee orientation. There are several reasons for this imperative:

- It reduces their anxiety.
- They "ramp up" quicker and become more efficient much quicker.
- They have decided to join you and accept the position, but they haven't decided to stay.

When you make a commitment to give an employee an orientation, they *feel appreciated*. I have worked for many companies in my career where I did not receive any orientation at all. I was provided with a desk and some cursory instructions to "Follow Fred around for a while—he will show you the ropes." I felt ill at ease, and it took me a while to get on my feet and figure out what was going on. This is not the feeling that you want a new employee to have! You want them to be confident, competent, and ready to work (more on employee orientation later in the book).

Chapter Two: Defining and Leveraging Training

When an employee moves into a new position. When an employee moves into a new role, he or she will need new knowledge and new skills. This is when training is essential: so that they have a high chance of succeeding in their new role. The training can be provided by the person who is vacating the role, if it is appropriate. No matter who is doing the training, however, there needs to be a specific structure and process, as well as accountability.

When there is a performance problem. Many times an employee is failing because they want to do well in their role but have not been given the proper training. (Translation: They don't know how to do their job.) I once worked in a retail store as part of the "management development program." Most of the time I was thrown into tasks I didn't know how to do. I was asked to fire someone without any training on how to have that kind of discussion and I was asked to do financial reports without any training in how to do them. The list goes on. I can tell you this: I was not a very good assistant manager, and I often felt off-balance and incompetent. When an employee is failing, try to determine if it is because of attitude, lack of knowledge, or lack of skill. Then try to help them out. It is also important to position your response as a positive action instead of punishment.

When it is part of their individual development plan (IDP). Every employee should have an individual development plan—a development plan that is aligned with the employee's long-term goals and arrived at during the employee's annual IDP meeting (which is separate from their annual performance review). Once both parties have agreed on the skills or knowledge that needs to be developed, then it is the obligation of the leader to provide training and development. This should be done for *every* employee, not just managers and supervisors. There is a great reason for this: if everyone on your team is getting individual development, your productivity will increase and there will be opportunities to identify talent that has, up until now, been undiscovered. Someone in an administrative role, for example, might have an interest in being part of management someday. Develop that person and everyone discovers a "diamond in the rough." It happens every day in corporate America by accident. As a leader, don't make it an accident! Be proactive, and find new talent within the organization. The current CEO of International House of Pancakes was at one time a server.

When there is massive change going on in the organization. If your company, your division, and your team is in the midst of upheaval, train them how to handle it. Let them take the training as a group; this allows them to have in-depth discussions about the problems and challenges they are facing, and will help them develop strategies. They'll feel more at ease and more prepared to survive the changes as they happen.

When there are new products, processes, or procedures. If you introduce a new piece of software, train people in how to use it. If a new product is being rolled out, let the employees learn about it *before* the customer. If new HR policies are being implemented, have a training for that new roll-out. I once worked for a company during the roll-out of a new phone system. They arranged for the sales representative to run around the office and give everybody a lesson in how to operate it. When she came to my office, she spent all of 10 dizzyingly fast minutes with me, and then bolted to meet with the next person. For months, people were disconnecting calls when they tried to transfer them and were befuddled by the many buttons on their consoles and what they meant.

When you need to build bench strength as part of succession planning. Every organization, big or small, will need talent in the future—supervisors, managers, and executives in every department. The big question is this: Do you hire them from outside, or build from within? I personally believe that it is good to have a mix of both. The advantage of developing internal talent

Chapter Two: Defining and Leveraging Training

is that if someone leaves, you can fill the spot quickly because you already have someone in the company who can replace them. (If you have to hire someone, it may take months to run through the process.) Training that is well designed and strategic can identify and help develop a group of "high potentials" and get them ready for increases in responsibilities down the line. It's like being the coach of a football team: You don't need a great quarterback when your star goes down with an injury—you need a great quarterback that you have developed on second string, who has been ready all along.

When they ask for it. Am I saying that training should be provided for anyone on your team who asks? Am I saying you should send someone to Harvard for the $10,000 leadership program just because they ask? Yes and no. Most people who ask to be trained are excited and feel that they have a need for the training. Are there exceptions—people who want to go because the training is in Bermuda or at Disney? That happens sometimes. However, most people ask for training because they sincerely want or need it. If that is the case, you should grant the wish as long as they need the skills or knowledge for their current or future job, you have the budget available to send them, there are no better and cheaper resources, and this person isn't asking for training every week. Knowing that their employer is investing in them is a tremendous motivator for most employees. If you can do it, it will make a world of difference.

Now you know what training is and have an idea as to when people should be trained. Here are 10 tips to leverage training to the greatest extent:

The Manager's Pocket Guide to Training

Make Training Work for You:
10 Tips

1. **Whenever you meet as a group, train.** Whenever you have an on-site or off-site meeting, try to make training a part of the meeting. You already have people there and the money is already being spent, so why not? I've worked for many leaders who made training a part of every local, divisional, regional, or national meeting. Most of the meetings included some "business meetings," some recreation, an award ceremony, and always training. Here is another compelling reason: If it is a meeting, then in theory the money doesn't have to come out of your training budget!

2. **Get a vendor to pay for it.** Believe it or not, many vendors have budgets for client training. I once met with a prospective client who told me that a very large computer company was paying to have a sales training company come in and train its salespeople. Their philosophy was that if the salespeople sell better, they will sell more of the product. (If you don't ask, you don't get.)

3. **Apply for a grant.** Many states have grant money waiting to be spent on training. This is free money provided by the state in order to build skills for residents of the state. The thought is that if employees have better skills, companies will be more successful, hire more people, and generate more tax revenue. In my state, the three most-funded categories for training are technical training, leadership development, and workforce skills (soft skills). I know of companies that have been able to land up to $500,000 in grant money. Here is the catch: It is a complicated and laborious application process. You can find out more by contacting your state and asking them who underwrites the grants in the state—possibly community colleges or individual companies that have been approved by the state. You can apply for grants and have someone on your staff do all the paperwork and administrative jumping through hoops, or you can have an outside company do all the work for you. (I recommend this latter approach, because fees for their services are worth the savings in labor, and these people are experts who can maximize the amount of the grant.)

(continued)

Chapter Two: Defining and Leveraging Training

Make Training Work for You
10 Tips *(continued)*

4. **Go back to school.** Many colleges and universities have the ability to assess, design, and conduct training to meet your needs—often at fairly reasonable rates. Contact them and set up a meeting to explain what you are looking for. Some educational institutions even have departments that specialize in dealing with and meeting the needs of corporate or small-business clients.

5. **Locate and use internal resources and talent.** In my opinion, every organization has untapped and unused talent that can be leveraged. There are people in your organization whose background or experience will be useful, such as people who have taught public speaking who are not assigned to your training department. There are people who not only know how to sell brilliantly, but can teach the art of selling to others. There is a wealth of information residing within the company (and not just in Human Resources or Training). I once attended a great presentation on negotiating taught by an attorney from the Legal department. It makes perfect sense, doesn't it? Ask colleagues and people who are in the know. You'll uncover resources you didn't know you had. Here is a bonus—the cost is often almost nothing, because they are already on the organization's payroll!

6. **Build your own training library.** Have someone on staff buy a wide assortment of training DVDs and audio CDs on a variety of soft-skill topics. (They can get great deals when they buy in volume from suppliers.) Let everyone on the team know they are available; when managers think someone needs brushing up on a topic, they can just have them review the latest DVD. There has to be someone keeping track of "check-in" and "check-out," which can be time consuming and labor intensive, but it's a one-time cost, and DVDs can be used for many people—kind of like a local in-office version of Blockbuster!

(continued)

> **Make Training Work for You**
> **10 Tips** *(concluded)*
>
> 7. **Budget for training.** Great organizations budget for training every year. The budget for training is based on an overall long-term training plan for each department or division, in areas such as skills training, technical training, or leadership development. You'll have to have top-level commitment within the organization, and long-term commitment and thinking.
>
> 8. **Hire a top-notch training expert.** Many companies hire a manager or director of training to design, implement, and worry about training 24/7. The advantage of having someone who is an expert is that he or she knows suppliers and resources that will save you time, energy, and money. If you don't want to add a staff member for training responsibilities, hire a consultant who is an expert in training and development to fill the role on an as-needed basis.
>
> 9. **Look to outside resources.** There are training companies that travel around the country giving seminars and national training companies known for specific skills (i.e., sales training, negotiating, or leadership). A local training company or an individual trainer or consultant might be all you need (more on this in a subsequent chapter).
>
> 10. **Think unconventionally.** Instead of always thinking of training in the conventional manner, do something different. For example, even an article from a magazine about a specific business issue or challenge can be turned into a training opportunity if it is discussed as a group. So stop thinking of training and think about something very simple: How can your people *learn*?

Ultimately it is the responsibility of the leader to make sure that training is used *effectively and efficiently* in order to get results. As Harvey Firestone, founder of Firestone Tire and Rubber Company, once said, "The growth and development of people is the highest calling of leadership."

A worksheet to help you think through ways to leverage training and come up with specific actions follows.

Chapter Two: Defining and Leveraging Training

Training Paths	Ask these questions:	Action Items
Whenever you meet as a group, train.	• What meetings are we having this year? • Which ones would be good to use for training? • Why?	
Get a vendor to pay for it.	• Which vendors should we approach? • Which ones represent mutually beneficial win-wins? • Who does enough business to justify it?	
Apply for a grant.	• Is a grant possible? • Which states would we apply to for grants? • In what categories? • If we could get grant money, what training areas would we spend more on? • What local resources can help us with grants?	
Go back to school.	• Which colleges in the area have programs for corporate clients? • Which community colleges have them? • Which four-year schools have them? • Who can get this information?	
Locate internal resources and talent.	• Who can I contact in HR to talk about internal talent? • Is there a Training department? • Which other departments can help? • Who else can I ask? • What kind of information do I need?	

(continued)

(concluded)

Training Paths	Ask these questions:	Action Items
Build your own training library.	• What topics do I need information on for my team? • What skills do I want to zero in on? • Who can do the research and find suppliers? • How much can I budget for this? And when? • Who will oversee the purchase and manage the materials?	
Budget for training.	• What budget do we have for training? • Do we have a budget for IT training? • Do we have a budget for soft-skills training? • Do we have a budget for leadership training and development? • What percentage of revenue can I budget? • Any other line item budget amounts available?	
Hire a top-notch training expert.	• Do I want to hire a person to oversee training? An employee or a consultant? • What do I want this person to do short, mid, and long term? • What is my budget for this kind of talent? • What can I expect my costs to be?	

Chapter Three
How People Learn

Sit back and think through one very important question: How do people learn? The last time you learned something, what was it? How did you learn it? Did you read a book? Watch a DVD? Learn it from a friend? Go to a seminar? Review information online? Or did you learn on the job or through trial and error?

It is critical that you understand how we human beings learn. If you are a leader, you might not actually conduct the training or even oversee the training, but I want to be crystal clear about this: you must—*absolutely must*—have a general understanding about how people learn so that you can make intelligent decisions about training.

How do people learn?

There is a lot of information out there that is just plain not true (and often dangerous). Complete this short survey to see what misinformation accidentally got through to you and then read on from there.

How People Learn		
How do people learn? Circle "T" for true and "F" for false for each statement.		
Most people learn by being taught.	T	F
The best way to learn is to read.	T	F
The best way to learn is to do.	T	F
The best way to learn is to listen.	T	F
Formal training works better than informal.	T	F
Students who are attentive, quiet, and sedentary learn more.	T	F
Learning is more effective in a group.	T	F
Learning has a direct correlation to IQ.	T	F
Learning can be self-driven.	T	F
Most people learn more when they are motivated.	T	F

How did you do? The correct answers are below.

These are trick questions—there are no correct answers. Sorry about that, but I wanted you to start thinking about this topic first. So here is the first key point: There is no one right way for all individuals to learn. As soon as we say that people learn a certain way, there will be notable exceptions. We do know a few key things about adult learning and what works and what doesn't. Here are some of these important concepts about learning that you must know.

Involvement drives learning and retention. Think about why I asked you to complete the little survey on the previous page: I wanted you to be involved—not just reading, but *doing*. When we were in kindergarten, we learned by doing. We cut out paper. We pasted words on the paper and colored them in. We made sculptures and models. We made up songs and poems. Am I saying we should do that now? Maybe! The brilliant teachers we had in kindergarten knew how to keep us involved and stimulated. We grow up, and suddenly the world thinks we can learn by attending a meeting where we sit listening to lectures for eight hours. We fight like crazy to stay awake and attentive in case someone asks us a question, but what we're really thinking about is the next break, snack, or lunch. What happened? If people are to learn (and the last time I checked, this was one of the goals of training), they need to be involved. For example, if adults are supposed to learn a leadership concept, can they get it through a lecture? Or is it better for them to engage in a discussion with the facilitator, and follow up with a case study in small groups, where everyone can be involved and work to solve and report on their results? See the difference?

People learn by doing. How did you learn to ride a bicycle? How did you learn to drive? In a classroom? No, you simply learned to drive *by driving*. I have seen so many people in the classroom "get" a new skill (let's say how to sell and demonstrate a new

Chapter Three: How People Learn

product) *intellectually*. The trainer would then say, "Okay, does everybody have it?" to a collective "Yes." One wise facilitator said, "Okay, so now each one of you is going to practice it in pairs, while I observe." The room falls apart. Why? Because people knew what the concept was, but hadn't really learned how to apply it. After practicing, they would often say, "Wow! I learned so much I didn't realize!" So here is the key point of all key points: If you want people to learn, it's okay to tell them and have them read and study about it, but the real learning happens when they actually *do* it. It's the difference between watching an interview being conducted, and being the person doing the interview. So no matter if it is group training or one-on-one training, always make sure they do it and get feedback and then do it again.

When learning is fun, people learn more. Do you remember the last time you participated in training? Do you remember how much fun it was? You don't? Sorry. Let me suggest that if the training had been fun, you would have remembered more about it. When people are having fun, they learn more! Think of your best high school teacher. Didn't he or she make it fun? In our fast-paced, overly stimulated and entertained society, training has to be fun, or people will get bored and mentally check out. I have incorporated everything you can imagine to make training fun over the years. I once turned a four-hour training session into a Wheel of Fortune–type game show. I felt I had to do something, because it was a product-knowledge training—already a boring topic. Use props, pictures, custom videos, and every exercise or game you can think of for the topic. Understand this: It is not silly or fun *just for the sake of being* fun. It is for driving retention and increasing the learning.

People learn when it is relevant to their job or current situation. I have a friend whose dad is a security guard. The hospital he works for decided that every employee should attend a 12-week "Personal Mission Vision and Values" workshop—one class each week for 12 weeks. The guards thought it was, and I quote, "a big waste of time." The hospital's executives were well intentioned—I am sure they wanted to provide the guards with something that would benefit them personally and professionally. The problem was that the guards didn't see it as that, and they just shut down. Your challenge as a leader is to make sure your people get training that is relevant, convince them that it is relevant, and *help them see why*.

Learning is a choice. If employees decide that they don't want to learn or they don't need to learn, they just won't.

People learn differently. You notice Fred sitting in the corner of a U-shaped table during the training session. He is being quiet, and you see that he is carefully taking his pen apart and putting it back together again in different configurations. Should we assume that he is not paying attention, or that he is not engaged? No. In fact, he might be very engaged, and this is how he learns. Some people learn better in a group, and some learn better on their own. Some learn better reading, and some learn better listening. Some people don't like reading. Be *very careful* not to assume that how you learn is how others learn as well.

Learning takes time. You hold your training class on Friday, all day long—eight hours on a specific topic. So everyone has learned and is ready to roll on Monday, right? Nope. Just because they were exposed to information doesn't mean that they learned it. It only means that there was exposure. In fact, most research indicates that the first time we're exposed to information, we only retain about 15 to 20 percent. It is now up to you and them to figure out how they can learn and retain 100 percent of it. Learning takes time.

Learning is cultural. In every organization, there is a degree of commitment and understanding as to the importance of learning. Some organizations say they really value training, but it's just talk. Other organizations say it and mean it, and back it up. The

Chapter Three: How People Learn

team quickly picks up on how important learning really is to the organization. The leader of the team sends the message; he or she says, "Hey Cindy! I know you wanted to go to that training tomorrow, but we are really busy, so I am going to pull you out." Message sent: We are busy. Message received: It doesn't matter that much. So it is up to you to set a learning culture.

Learning Styles

Every leader must know about learning styles and be able to recognize them. Each of us is born with or adapts to a learning style that we have a preference for. We may not even be aware of it, but it exists.

There are three main learning styles: visual, auditory, and kinesthetic. Most of us learn in all three ways and even have a preference for one specific style, but there are many people who can only learn one way. Let's look at these learning styles in a little more detail by focusing on the learner.

The "visual" learner. Visual learners learn by seeing the world. They learn by reading and seeing pictures, diagrams, illustrations, and so on. Visual learners tend to love video and even slide shows or PowerPoint presentations. They love movies and anything primarily visual. This preference is even reflected in the words they use: *"Oh Jim, I see your point." "I look at it this way . . ." "I get the picture now—oh wow!" "From my point of view . . ."*

The "auditory" learner. Auditory learners learn and understand by hearing the world. They learn by listening to people talk. Lectures, speeches, and audio recordings are helpful learning tools. Auditory learners love anything that appeals to the ear, such as music and radio programs. Their preference is also reflected in the words they use: *"I hear you." "I can relate to what Pete is saying." "That is a sound idea." "What I heard Betty saying is that . . ."*

The "kinesthetic" learner. Kinesthetic learners learn through physical activity and direct involvement. They are the ones who learn about lawn mowers by taking the engine apart and reassembling it again. They want to *do*—not sit and watch. They make great scribes in training classes because they get to do something. They will say things like: *"Yes, this idea has a nice feel to it." "I need to get a handle on this situation." "This needs to be locked down." "I think we need to grab this by the horns."*

Most people do tend to learn better with one approach, but keep in mind that two or more approaches work best for others who adapt to the world around them. Training and learning will be more effective if the person doing the training combines auditory, visual, and kinesthetic approaches. Don't take the risk of having someone tune out or have a hard time absorbing the information because of the way the program is designed. It's critical that you understand this reality.

Let's see how well you have absorbed the lesson.

In the following chart, write down which kind of learner would respond well to the presentation mode listed in the column to the left: visual, auditory, or kinesthetic.

Chapter Three: How People Learn

Learning Mode	Appeals to what kind of learner?
PowerPoint presentation	
PowerPoint with audio	
A written exercise	
Activity where people build a tower from straws	
Writing ideas down on an index card	
Answering questions in a group discussion	
Sponge ball thrown around the room as people answer questions	
Watching a DVD	
Listening to music while individually developing ideas on paper	
Writing an idea on a sticky note and posting it on a chart	
Working with a partner on a problem and presenting the solution to the group	

See how this works? Did you also notice that some of these activities or modes are likely to appeal to more than one kind of learner? For example, a PowerPoint presentation with audio might appeal to both the visual learner and the auditory learner, whereas using sticky notes and charts might appeal to the visual learner and the kinesthetic learner. (Note to the reader: This little exercise just got the involvement of the visuals and the kinesthetics!) If you can combine modes, even more learning will take place. You're not having an exercise for the sake of having an exercise, or having a video for the sake of having a video; you're making sure that more learning takes place that involves all the styles. If I am producing a video, I am going for great visuals—I am going to have some great music in the background and have workbooks or pads that someone can take notes on. I want to appeal to *all the learning styles*.

A smart trainer will stop the video every now and then and ask participants to discuss what they have learned so far. Why do that? To get the auditory people involved!

Accelerated Learning

So now that you have a general understanding of the ways people learn, it's time to learn how to make the learning even more effective. What if you could increase retention by as much as 50 percent? You can, with accelerated learning, which dramatically increases the effectiveness and retention of information.

Georgi Lozanov, a Bulgarian professor of psychiatry and psychotherapy, came up with the concept through research in foreign language training. He used music, visuals, and other materials that would stimulate the senses. Lozanov found that when he involved the senses in the training regimen, the retention rate went up dramatically.

According to Bobbi DePorter, author of *Quantum Learning,* the basic theories as it relates to accelerated learning are these:

- Learning is dual-planned or para-conscious. We learn through our conscious and our subconscious mind.

- Everything makes a suggestion, either consciously or unconsciously. A student might consciously be listening to the teacher, but subconsciously his mind is aware of the peripherals: the teacher's mood, tone of voice, and noises in the room.

- There is no single stimulus. The way we receive or perceive information is in context.

Chapter Three: How People Learn

- Everything is constantly being processed by our brain, including symbols, rituals, and associations.
- There is no neutral information, only positive or negative. Teachers need to make a concerted effort to create as many positives as possible, paying careful attention to creating a safe and fun learning environment.

What conclusions can you draw from this information? We as leaders need to make sure we incorporate all of these principles in our work—not "just because," but in order to really drive learning. Here are some key points to consider when you set up a training course:

- **Who is the teacher, the facilitator, or the leader?**
- **Be careful who you select as the teacher, trainer, or facilitator.** Many companies don't take their time to find the right person. The trainer is the program. Great content and an unskilled facilitator is still an awful program, but an "okay" program with a great facilitator might turn out to be a great program, because a professional facilitator knows how to make it better. Let me give you an example: I once facilitated a program in Nashville, Tennessee, for a group of about 50 people. All the arrangements for the hotel and the meeting room were made by the client, and I had no control over selection of the location. The hotel was an absolute dump—the rooms were awful, and the meeting room was shabby. On the morning of an eight-hour session, the participants were all in a bad mood. I said "Good morning," and all I got were glares. Here is what I said next: "Does everybody hate this hotel? (They all said yes.) "Does everybody hate this room?" (They all said yes.) Then I said, "I do, too. None of us had control over where we are, so we have a decision to make. Do we want to have a *productive day,* or a nonproductive

day?" They agreed to make the best of it, and we moved on. A less-experienced facilitator would have chosen to ignore the situation, and the day would have been ruined.

- **Look at all the elements**. Everything counts: the room, the chairs, the visuals, the handouts, the posters, the food, the temperature. *It all matters!* I've trained all around the country and have seen pitiful training rooms within corporations that send a terrible message: beat-up paneling, old dirty chairs, and scarred walls say, *This isn't important—it doesn't matter.* On the other hand, I've been in companies that had magnificent training facilities that were just top notch. People came in feeling good and excited even before the session started! Think about the message that your meeting/training room is sending. If the response is *It's expensive to modify this room,* then go to a hotel.

Let's see how you rate various elements in the training environment.

Chapter Three: How People Learn

The Training Environment

Instructions: Rate each item as it relates to the training you plan, conduct, or participate in, using the scale of 1–5 (1 = the worst; 5 = the best).

We have highly skilled facilitators.	1	2	3	4	5
We have world-class content.	1	2	3	4	5
We have training that addresses the different learning styles.	1	2	3	4	5
We have a dedicated space for training.	1	2	3	4	5
The space is well lit.	1	2	3	4	5
The space has comfortable chairs.	1	2	3	4	5
The space has all the proper AV equipment.	1	2	3	4	5
Training is fun most of the time.	1	2	3	4	5
Training is interactive.	1	2	3	4	5
Food is provided for all-day sessions.	1	2	3	4	5
The food is of high quality.	1	2	3	4	5
Pre-training communication "pre-sells" the value.	1	2	3	4	5
Music is part of our training program.	1	2	3	4	5
Handout materials are of high quality.	1	2	3	4	5
Our content is always relevant.	1	2	3	4	5
The content is always of high quality.	1	2	3	4	5
We have lots of exercises, discussions, and other activities in the training.	1	2	3	4	5
We provide plenty of breaks during training.	1	2	3	4	5
We have students do pre-work before they come to the training.	1	2	3	4	5
The space has nice functional tables.	1	2	3	4	5
Total for each column					

Grand Total (add column scores)

(Scoring interpretation is on the next page.)

39

Interpretation of Training Environment Results

Since there are 20 statements, it is possible to earn a perfect score of 100, but there aren't many perfect people. How well did you rate on environmental factors?

100–90   Great job! You are really looking after all of the elements that relate to training.

89–80   You did okay and for the most part, you are fairly strong in setting up a good training environment. However, there are a few elements you need to look at and modify.

79–70   Well, you probably could use some help. You'll need to put some time into this and examine all the desired elements in training. Put some plans together to fix them.

69 and below: Red alert! You are in a crisis situation when it comes to training. Seek immediate expert help.

♦ ♦ ♦ ♦ ♦ ♦ ♦ ♦

Positioning Your Training as a "Win"

One way to make training much more effective is to make sure that it is positioned properly. Most companies do not seem to pay attention to the way the program is described to participants who are going to be attending. Let me give you a few examples.

I once went to Queens, New York, to conduct a training session for a company with an outside sales force. I arrived that morning quite excited about doing the training. The group was somewhat resistant in the morning, and I couldn't understand why. During a break, one of the participants said to me, "Well, we weren't too thrilled today about coming to the session." When I asked her why, she explained that she received a letter from her boss saying that everyone had to attend the session or they would be fired. This set up a very negative situation from the start.

Chapter Three: How People Learn

Another time, I was ready to conduct a training session for managers. The managers arrived in the training room and did not appear to be hostile, but they did seem a little disoriented and confused. When I asked them at the beginning of the session what they wanted to get out of the program, they said that they didn't know because they weren't even told what the program was going to be about! They had been kept in the dark, and just told to show up.

Attitude is an often-overlooked and underestimated aspect of training, and it is important to remember that it is developed *before* the training happens. Here are my top 12 recommendations for positioning the training as a win:

---

12 Recommendations for Positioning the Training

1. **Communicate the purpose of the training in advance.** Make sure that every participant knows the purpose of the training and why it is being held at this time.
2. **Sell the benefits of the training.** Be sure to sell the benefits of the training and how it will benefit participants specifically. (For example, you can say in your advance communication, "This leadership program is a top-notch program and I know it will benefit everyone by helping you acquire new skills and make their leadership tasks a little easier.")
3. **Sell the program content.** What makes this content valuable and relevant? (For example, you might say, "I have done lots of research and attended many programs, and this is the top program in the world on this topic. It is world-class.")
4. **Sell the facilitator.** It is important to sell the facilitator's qualifications and background in order to build a real excitement about the course. You can mention their background, credentials, and experience as it relates to the topic.
5. **Make it personal.** The communication about the training should be addressed to each person in an e-mail or a letter. It should not be a blanket e-mail to all people, if possible.

(continued)

The Manager's Pocket Guide to Training

12 Recommendations for Positioning the Training *(continued)*

6. **Make it special.** Let people who are attending know why the training is special. Is it exclusive? Expensive? Limited to a certain number of people? Only for a certain department? In a great location?
7. **Have the communication come from an executive.** If the communication comes from an executive who is higher up the ladder, it signifies a higher level of importance.
8. **Keep it positive.** Don't position the training as a negative event, even if it is for negative reasons. (Let's say sales are down 50 percent over the year before. Don't say, "Sales are way down, so we are having training." Say, "I know that you are all talented and smart and I want to make sure you are all hitting your numbers this year and reaching your goals. I have decided to invest some time and money in training that I think we can all benefit from for the rest of this year. I think you will find the session to be fun, useful, and well worth your time.")
9. **Take a survey.** Send a survey or a questionnaire in advance of the session and ask participants questions about what they want out of the training. This can create a little positive "buzz" about the training. Here are some questions you may want to include in the survey:

   Why do you want to attend this training session?
   What do you want to get out of the program?
   What are your biggest challenges as it relates to _____?
   What are three topics you would like to have covered?
   How do you think this program would help our team?
   How do you think this program would help our company?
   What time would be the ideal start time for you?
   Do you prefer frequent breaks more often, or longer breaks less often?
   Do you prefer a 45-minute lunch and a slightly shorter day, or a 1-hour lunch and a slightly longer day?

(continued)

Chapter Three: How People Learn

12 Recommendations for Positioning the Training *(continued)*

10. **Communicate logistics.** Far too many programs start off in confusion because of poor pre-session communication. People need to know:
    - When the session is being held.
    - Where it is being held, *with clear directions*. (I have seen many session-communication letters that have said something like "The session is in triad B in room T1065." Am I supposed to know where that is located?)
    - What time the session starts—*really* starts. (Some memos I have seen have said "Start at 8:00," and the session actually starts at 9:00 a.m. with breakfast at 8:00 a.m. What if you don't eat breakfast?)
    - What should they bring? (A pen? A notebook? A pre-assignment? Reports of some kind? Tell them.)
    - What time will the session end? (Many people have child-care issues and need to know in advance.)
    - Dress attire. (How should they dress? Should they be in business attire or business casual? If one of those categories, what does that mean? I have found business casual can mean many things to many people.)
    - Meals. Will they be provided? What should they do if they have special requirements?
    - Contacts. (Who should they contact if they have questions or a problem?)
    - Travel. (What are the details, and who is handling that?)
    - Lodging. (Where are they staying, and who is handling that?)

(continued)

> **12 Recommendations for Positioning the Training** *(concluded)*
>
> 11. **Make it by invitation only.** Have a training that is available only to people with a certain level of performance, or who have been promoted to a certain level, or who have applied and been accepted into "the program." (I once was in charge of the leadership development program for a large division of a Fortune 100 company. I set up a leadership development program for employees who wanted to eventually become a leader in the company. We communicated out to the field that this was an elite program and only a select amount of people would be admitted to the program each year. (Out of 1,200 employees in this division and only 50 would be admitted into the program. For admission consideration, they had to take a leadership assessment and complete a ten-page, essay-style application. The information packets were reviewed, and an objective point system was applied to evaluate candidates and rank them. After all was said and done, 47 people were admitted into the program. They received this great news in a very impressive letter written by the head of the division. When the program started, the participants were very excited because they were part of a very exclusive program and they had won! They felt special just to be there.)
>
> 12. **Use the session introduction to build enthusiasm for the training.** I was facilitating a one-day session at a very large company, and there were about 45 people in the room. I asked the leader of the group if she wanted to do an introduction of the session and introduce me. Her reply was "No, just go ahead. We aren't real big on introductions." That is a huge strategic error: The introduction is the *last chance* to position the training program before it gets started. I have also seen introductions from leaders that were so poor and so unenthusiastic that they might as well not have happened. An introduction should be short and it should build excitement for the session as well as pre-sell the benefits.

Timing is everything!

One of the factors that many people overlook is *timing*. Poor timing can make or break a training session! (This seems to be an area that many leaders just don't think about at all.) Here are

Chapter Three: How People Learn

some tips to make sure that the schedule doesn't have a negative impact on training and, more importantly, on *learning:*

It's all in the Timing

The goal is to provide training, not to kill them! I have seen training that went from 7:00 a.m. to 7:00 p.m. Let's think this through: Does it make sense to beat people up by having training that lasts 12 hours? It's utter nonsense! The leaders will say, however, that they are *trying to maximize the investment* or *make good use of time.* The reality is that it is a horrible use of time and is actually counter-productive, because at some point, people can only absorb so much. Start training at a reasonable time (8:30 or 9:00 a.m.) and end at a reasonable time (no later than 4:00 p.m.). Going beyond that just ruins retention. The other point is that you want to give people time to think!

Skip the temptation to shorten lunch or work through lunch. I have seen many a training session where lunch is shortened from one hour to 45 minutes to 30 minutes. This is done in an effort to save time or make up time. This is just plain wrong and wrong-minded; people need breaks to stretch their legs and refresh their minds. (Some groups strike a bargain with the facilitator and get lunch shortened in order to end earlier. This is no bargain, because it doesn't change the fact that the minds of the participants are still tired because they didn't get a long enough break at lunch!) Here is another benefit of taking a longer lunch: If the training is really well done, more times than not people at lunch are talking about the training and learning from one another! If this time is short-circuited, then the learning doesn't happen.

Avoid the graveyard shift. I have conducted many training sessions that were held between 3:00 and 5:00 p.m. (not by choice!). People in those sessions were tired from staying focused all day and had to really struggle to pay attention. Don't do this to yourself! Don't do this to them! It does them a great disservice. Have a break after 4:00 p.m. so that people can relax.

Do not, under any circumstances, skip breaks. Why do people skip breaks and shorten breaks? Do they think that participants don't have to go to the bathroom? Don't need to stretch? That smokers don't need to smoke? Skipping breaks is *disrespectful* to the individuals in the group who have biological and physical needs.

(continued)

45

The Manager's Pocket Guide to Training

It's all in the Timing *(concluded)*

Think about the day of the week. What days are best or worst for your team? The participants in one of my training sessions told me that their management had scheduled the class on the day that was their busiest. The session would automatically put them behind, creating a situation where everyone was thinking more about their workload than the training. Some days work better than others: Wednesdays are often a good choice, because people have two days to catch up on their work before and two days to catch up on work after. Fridays are also good, because it "feels" like a break in routine (especially if it is an off-site meeting). (Some participants have a more open mindset on Fridays than they do the rest of the week. Monday is usually the worst day for training.)

Think about the time of year. There are certain times of the year that make training difficult because it is hard to get everyone to attend. The summer months are sometimes slow, but July and August are almost always filled with vacations. The holidays around Thanksgiving and Christmas are always a challenge in terms of scheduling. In some areas, winter months are tough times to schedule training because of weather-related difficulties.

A short tool to help you think through when you want to plan your training programs follows.

Scheduling Our Training

The best hours to conduct training in this organization are:

The best time to schedule lunch: (11:30, 12:00, 1:00)
Important considerations:

Number of breaks and times:

The days of the week that work best for me and the organization:
    Blackout days:
    Important considerations:

The best times of the year to schedule training:
    Blackout days:
    Important considerations:

Other timing considerations specific to the organization
(e.g., busy season, trade shows, vacations, holidays):

The Importance of Fun in Training

I'm always amazed when participants are surprised and delighted that training is fun. This tells me that there must be a lot of training going on out there that is not fun and in fact is dry and boring and stodgy. There is no rule I know of that says that training has to be dry and boring and stodgy. In fact, making training fun will increase retention and make it energetic, memorable, and just plain buzz-worthy. So make sure not to overlook the critical importance of fun as part of the training.

Chapter Four
Types of Training

The purpose of this chapter is to outline the kinds of training that are available to organizations. When most people think of training, they think of one thing—the classroom. When they hear the word *learning,* what comes to mind is usually something different. I want you to move beyond standard thinking and start thinking about the variety of methods available to any organization that wants to focus on learning.

Classroom Training

Classroom training is by far the most popular method. It is effective and useful when you want to teach skills, concepts, and principles in large groups. Everyone has had some experience in a classroom and knows how it works. It can either be conducted by someone on staff or someone hired externally. There are some advantages to classroom training:

Advantages of Using Classroom Training

It is effective for developing skills. Classroom training often involves role plays and practice so that learners will have a chance to apply or demonstrate their skills and get feedback on the spot.

It builds a sense of team and esprit de corps. Groups that go through training together tend to develop a sense of team spirit and connection that carries over to the workplace when the training is over.

It is effective. A classroom setting makes it possible to train several people at once (up to 50 to 60 people). In one week, you can train as many as 300 learners.

It is interactive. Participants are able to learn from one another, thus enhancing the training itself.

Disadvantages of Using Classroom Training

Individual training needs are not always met. The pace of the training has to be in line with the entire group; if one person is struggling with the material, the facilitator can't slow down the pace too much.

It is easy for people to *not* be involved. If there are a large number of people in the class, those who don't want to be there are not likely to actively participate. I am often approached by managers who ask about specific participants. I have to scratch my head and say that I don't know because Diana or Bob or Jason was quiet throughout the class and basically blended into the woodwork.

It can be very expensive. The cost of conducting training at an outside facility is often high when the company has to pay for room rental, food, audio/visual services, the printing of participant guides, and so on.

It is time-consuming. It can take several days to teach a subject in a classroom setting. Learners attending the training are out of their job function for that time as well, so there is lost production time.

It is not easily customizable. A class is designed for a group of people with similar needs. When the group taking the class changes and the material needs to reflect those changes, changing the materials, visuals, and exercises is laborious and might not even be possible.

The outcome can't be guaranteed. There are several components that can affect the outcome: (1) The facilitator might not perform well. (2) There might be bad chemistry between the facilitator and the group. (3) The course design might be inappropriate for the group. (4) One or more participants might be disruptive.

The course might not be available when you need it. A learner might need training on a certain topic immediately, but will have to wait until it is offered again on the schedule.

E-learning

E-learning has become very popular over the past decade. Some companies are replacing traditional training with e-learning, which allows individuals to take the training right at their computer, when it is convenient for them. Some companies claim to have saved millions from this approach. I am sure some have, but others have really disappointed learners by abandoning more traditional forms in favor of more e-learning. E-learning has pluses and minuses.

Advantages of Using E-learning

It is immediate. E-learning is immediately available to individuals anywhere, anytime. All you need is a computer connection.

It can be customized. Because the topics offered are such a wide range, topics can be selected by the learner and their manager.

It can be taken in parts. E-learning can be bookmarked so that a participant can stop when they have to and resume when they have more time.

It is very visual. E-learning appeals to the visual learner because it uses animation and color, as well as pictures.

It can be a great pre-learning assignment for a class. Participants can go online and complete a pre-class assignment *before* coming to class.

Learners can pick and choose. Most e-learning courses allow the learner to skip chapters and only concentrate on what they want or need to learn.

The learner is in control. Learners can decide when and where they want to learn. It puts them in control, unlike when they are taking a class.

Disadvantages of Using E-learning

It is not interactive. E-learning is not yet interactive. There are many e-learning companies that make the claim that their products are interactive, because people are asked to click here or click there and take quizzes. This is not interactive learning; it is a general one-way transaction where the course delivers information and the learner receives it.

It can be boring. I have seen many e-learning courses that absolutely put me to sleep, and I've seen others that are just books converted to an online format, with pages to read and click through. Yuck and double yuck.

It is hard to customize for each learner. (This is also an advantage, but for a different reason.) The content in an individual e-learning course is the same and can't be changed. Compare that to a live facilitator who can adjust to each learner's needs.

You can't practice and get feedback. With e-learning, you don't get the opportunity to practice and receive feedback. Yes, I have seen vendors that have simulations built into the e-learning—they are slick and provide some learning, but they are not the same as practicing with a real-live person.

It is dependent on technology. Technological problems having to do with firewalls, download speed, access to content, and so on

Chapter Four: Types of Training

will require tech support and assistance. The learners themselves will all have to have adequate technology in order to take part in the learning.

It raises HR concerns. Here is a scenario for you: Let's say a manager meets with an employee about performance and the two mutually decide that that employee will work on effective communication. They find a course in the wonderful e-learning library and sign up the employee. The employee is too busy during the workday to take the course, so he or she has to take it at home. Do you see the issue floating to the surface here? Here are the questions: Should that employee be paid for having to train at home? Should the employee be allowed time at work to take the e-learning course? If not, why not? Classroom learning is during work time, so you can see why this might be a problem.

It can be expensive. The development and roll out of e-learning are generally expensive and logistically laborious. There is the IT part of the equation, but also decisions about eligibility, registration, and so on. Many companies decide to develop some sort of learning management system to track who has taken each course and to store training data in a database, which adds considerably to the cost.

Self-Study

Self-study is highly effective in the right circumstances if it is used for the right reason. Studying on their own by reading or finding information online is probably the most overlooked method. A leader once asked me to improve my business communication skills. He asked me to locate a vendor or book and come back to him with recommendations. I found a correspondence course on business writing, and went to work. I had to study modules and write business letters, and submit them for review and evaluation by the company. Here is why it was self-study: (1) It was done on my own time. (2) It was private. (3) No one else was involved, with the exception of the company that had to send me critiques of my business writing.

Advantages of Using Self-Study

It is personal and can be highly customized. Since it is self-study, the learner with the leader's help can design a course of action that seems do-able. I once had an employee who decided to read a book about something he needed to improve on. We agreed on the book in advance, and I read the book as well. We met about every two weeks to discuss what he was learning and how he could apply it. This strategy was very effective for this particular individual.

It builds confidence and self-esteem. Self-study builds self-confidence because the learner receives positive attention. The fact that the manager is spending the time and energy on his or her development can be a great confidence-booster.

It is often very effective. Self-study is targeted and customized, so it is often very effective. Unlike classes or e-learning, there is only one person involved, so the development plan is focused and clear. There are no other people around to distract the learner either.

It is private. The advantage of self-study is it is private. Other people don't need to know what that person is learning, which is important for some people.

It is easy to track. It is easy to tell whether or not the learner is doing the assignment—there is no way someone can hide from the lesson being taught or escape accountability for the learning.

It is inexpensive. Self-study is very inexpensive, so it fits into almost any budget. Often times it involves only the cost of a book or an assessment, and the cost is for one or two copies at the most. Everyone in the department can be working on development needs each year. Making it a budgeted item also means that there is not likely to be resistance from upper management.

It is immediate. There is no waiting for a schedule or a next-time offering. The two parties can decide to start anytime.

Disadvantages of Using Self-Study

The manager has to know what to recommend. The learner's manager should know which resources will help the learner (book, article, Web site, etc.). Let's say the learner needs work in emotional intelligence; if the manager doesn't know about emotional intelligence or have any idea about resources to recommend, how can he track the learner's progress?

The self-study has to be clearly related to development in the eyes of the learner and the manager so it is not interpreted instead as punishment. It is essential that the manager explain *why* they want the learner to complete the self-study and how they think it will benefit the learner.

It requires discipline. When a manager and a learner decide on self-study as a learning strategy, there has to be a structured approach and a commitment for both parties to meet on the planned follow-up dates. Otherwise, the training initiative of self-study loses its importance. The learner thinks, *Well it must not be very important, because the words don't match the actions. My manager said it was important, but she hasn't even followed up with me.*

Outside Seminars

Outside seminars can be great sources of training if you don't have a training department or a good supplement to the training department. There are companies that offer seminars to the public on certain dates and times, and open up enrollment to the public.

Local community colleges also often offer seminars for non-credit. Contact your local Chamber of Commerce also, because such non-profits often sponsor training seminars of two hours or even full days as a service to their members.

One word of caution for all outside seminars: Watch for the dreaded "pitch training." This is when a company offers training packaged as training, but it is really a disguised sales pitch for their longer, more-expensive training programs. This practice is highly unethical, and you should avoid supporting them at all costs.

Advantages of Using Outside Training Seminars

Many are very good. The programs that are promoted and conducted around the country are good-to-excellent because they have been designed by professionals and rigorously tested. The other advantage is the trainers who conduct them are usually training veterans who know the material.

They are often targeted. The content of these kinds of programs is often narrow and specific, such as "How to Handle Conflict in the Workplace" or "How to be a Great Administrative Assistant."

They are centrally located. These kinds of seminars are usually easy to get to because the sponsors pick centralized locations, such as a major hotel with a conference room.

Reasonable in costs. These kinds of one-day seminars run between $129–$299 for the day (usually including a learner's guide and handouts).

Disadvantages of Using Outside Seminars

They are hit or miss. These sessions, while they are often good quality, can be terrible if they hire the wrong facilitator or the facilitator is having a bad day. (I have come across a few facilitators who were the worst).

Chapter Four: Types of Training

They can be too generic. The sessions are designed to fit across all industries and all levels of expertise, so the discussions at the session have to be general as well. Sometimes they are too general, and thus not as useful.

You can't control the mix of participants. Your employee can get stuck in a room full of participants who they don't want to be with for an hour, much less a day.

Sponsors often try to "up-sell." Many of these companies reward their facilitators with commissions when they "up-sell"— facilitators get paid if people enroll in additional classes right then and there or try to sell books and tapes. Employees are sometimes tempted to buy more, therefore give them some spending guidelines before they go so that they know what to do. (Setting the budget ahead of time will solve the problem.)

Videos and DVDs

There are many great video and DVD programs that are available on the open market on a million different topics. These can be useful tools and good ways to expose your teams to the ideas of well-known speakers and experts without having to pay them to appear personally. I have always had a good response when I've used them. (As an aside, HRD Press, the publisher of this book, makes available for purchase a wide assortment of excellent videos, and I am saying that because I am a fan. No one told me to!)

Advantages of Using Videos and DVDs

They are often timeless. Most video producers try to give their videos a long shelf life so that they don't look like outdated fads. The advantage here is that you can use the videos and DVDs for quite a long time before they look outdated.

The investment is a one-time investment. Once the material is purchased, it is the organization's to keep and use for any internal purpose.

They are usually well produced. The producers of most videos are pros who are pretty good at creating videos with good production value, good acting, and excellent content. They know how to add music and humor to make the production entertaining without looking tacky.

They are often accompanied by a leader's guide. Many videos come with a guide on ways to use the video and use the content as part of a training session. Some also offer participant guides as a separate purchase.

It is great material to build a meeting or training around. If you are looking for core information to build a meeting around, this is a great tool. Add exercises, discussion, and a good facilitator and you have the makings of a good training program!

Disadvantages of Using Videos and DVDs

There are bad videos out there. I've seen many truly awful videos that made me scratch my head and wonder why anyone would produce such an awful, stupid, inane video. Who thought it was good? Who decided to unleash it on an unsuspecting public? One word of caution: Never buy any video sight-unseen. Always preview it first.

When used improperly, a video can be deadly. I have seen trainers who say, "Okay, we are going to watch a video," shut down the lights, and sit at the back of the room. Videos used improperly and not introduced and set up correctly can put a group to sleep.

Chapter Four: Types of Training

They can interfere with interactivity. I have seen training where there were eight videos used in one day. That's way too many! You have to balance video and discussion and all the other elements we have talked about in this book.

The initial investment can be expensive. A high-quality DVD or video can run anywhere from $900 to $1,500. However, it can be a good investment in the long term if it is used to train many people over several years. Each time it is used, the cost of the investment goes down.

Equipment can sometimes be a problem. I know this sounds a little crazy, but I have seen many meetings where the facilitator could not get the VCR or the DVD player or the TV monitor to work, so they were not able to show the video or DVD at all.

Audio CDs

Instructional compact discs are also good resources for individualized or group training. Although it is not quite as effective as video, this media has its uses.

Advantages of Using Audio CDs

They are inexpensive. A CD or even a set of CDs can be used as part of a training session or for a sales meeting. They are also inexpensive.

They are content rich. These CDs are usually well produced and full of useful content.

Disadvantages of Using Audio CDs

They are not as interactive as many other methods. You eliminate the sight and have only the sound, so they are not as effective as other methods.

They can get boring fast. Make sure to play only the portions of an audio CD that are most relevant, and don't play them for more than 10 to 15 minutes at a stretch.

You have to decide which form of training is right for you, your team, and your organization as a whole. Educate yourself and get help from your HR or Training department, or ask an outside consultant to help you evaluate them. Also consider creating a training program that combines two or more methods.

Chapter Five
Sources for Training Delivery

In the previous chapter, we talked about methods of training. In this chapter the question to be answered is: *How can I find sources to help me deliver this stuff?* (By "stuff," we mean training programs.)

There are many internal and external sources. We'll outline the major ones.

The Human Resources Department

This is the gold mine of unknown sources. I've found HR to be particularly helpful in some areas:

Programs. Many programs and trainers are hidden away in the human resources department and are not well publicized. One company I worked for had a huge library of video and DVD programs that had never been used!

Speakers and consultants. HR departments often have contracts and contacts with outside trainers, facilitators, and speakers that they know from experience. Here is a little known fact: the HR department is often asked to provide elements for meetings, and often those elements are the training elements.

Talent. Because they are HR people, they usually know who in each department is a hidden resource or talent. Let me give you an example: I once needed a trainer for my Training department. I received a résumé from a staff person in Marketing who wanted the position. Huh? I called HR and asked them why I should interview a marketing person for a training position, when I needed someone with experience. I found out that this individual had been doing tons of training in her department, and might be the company's best-kept secret. HR people know where these resources are living in your organization.

Internal trainers. When you need an HR-related topic, this department might have someone internally who already has a program that fits your need (and who can do it tomorrow).

Training Department or Corporate University

This is so blatantly obvious it is scary, but let me tell you what is scarier: when you go out and spend money on an outside consultant, not realizing that you have a similar program in-house (almost free). I have seen so many situations where executives or leaders needed something and neglected to ask the Training department because they assumed it couldn't help. Here are some ways the Training department can help you:

Design and development. Training department people are usually delighted to help. They'll assess your needs and design a custom training program to meet those needs. I worked in these departments for 17 years, and let me tell you something: this is the kind of work that thrills the training professional. We love doing that kind of work from scratch! I designed more than 100 training programs throughout the years, and loved developing every last one of them.

Programs already in place. Most Training departments and corporate universities already have many programs developed and ready to roll. Contact them to find out what is available.

Resources available. Training departments have rosters of contractors, trainers, and consultants they've worked with and can make referrals. (They have tried out and eliminated other suppliers that didn't perform well—another advantage.)

Advice. Training departments can help you cost out and evaluate proposals and materials that outside companies send them.

Outside Consultants

Outside consultants can provide consultation, design, development, training facilitation, and a myriad of other services. Here is what they offer:

Expertise and experience. Consultants with years of experience can provide expertise that the internal organization does not have.

A different perspective. Consultants can see your problems from a more global perspective, because they don't just work with one client, but many. They in essence become aggregators of information.

Tools and processes. Many consultants have their own tools and processes that they use to get objective data for the project.

As-needed assistance. You can use consultants whenever you need them. When you don't need them, you don't have to pay anything.

Accessibility. Find consultants by contacting your local Chamber of Commerce, the American Society of Training and Development (www.astd.org), or the National Speakers Association (www.nsaspeaker.org). You can also find speakers and consultants in the local business listings.

Training Vendors

Many national and international training companies can come in and conduct the training or arrange to get one of your people certified. The way it works is that you find the program and try it out. If you like it, you select an employee to get certified. The company then puts that employee through their process to certify them. Usually, the employee has to experience the program as a student, attend some kind of certification training program, and teach a "pilot" program with your employees (someone from the training company observes). Such companies will charge a hefty fee for certification and a per-head cost for each student who goes through the program. The expense is the only disadvantage of this arrangement; you'll have to pay a certification fee and make minimum commitments in terms of the number of people who complete the program each year. Many ask for a multi-year contract.

"Red Flags"

When it comes to working with inside and outside resources, keep your antennae sharp. Here are some sure signs of trouble. Don't ignore any of them—something might be wrong.

A specific product or program is being pushed. Find out why an inside or an outside resource is pushing for a product or service. Pushing one product suggests that the company might be ignoring your needs (in my opinion, this is not professional). A consultant can make a recommendation, but he or she should back down if you don't accept it. Ultimately, you are the client and it is what you want that counts.

No needs assessment is done. The consultant should try to assess and uncover your needs *before* they make recommendations. A client called me to say that his team wasn't feeling so much like a team and he needed me to come in and do a one-day seminar to help them feel more like a team. After asking the client numerous questions on the phone, I then asked to interview a number of people of all levels before making a recommendation. After all, I really didn't know what the problem was, so I couldn't make a recommendation. It would be the equivalent of a doctor writing

Chapter Five: Sources for Training Delivery

a prescription without first examining the patient and making a diagnosis. If anyone attempts to recommend training without assessing first, look at it as a sign that they aren't being as thorough as they should be.

You're being asked to sign a multi-year contract with quantity minimums. Danger! This is when alarm bells should go off in your head. Vendors will tell you that multi-year contracts will save you money and guard against price increases, but what it really means is that the consultant wants to preserve his cash flow and revenue and obligate you to him. Here is a true story: I once signed a multi-year contract with a company that had minimum requirements. At the end of just one year, we had not met the minimum requirements and had to pay money back because we didn't make the numbers. It was a very difficult situation. I recommend one-year renewable contracts, which can make a difference.

There are upfront purchase requirements. Some outside companies require the upfront purchase of a minimum number of materials—perhaps 100 to 300 learner guides have to be purchased in advance and stored. I don't care for this approach for one reason: you might not use them all, and if there are changes (and there will be!), you will be stuck with them. I once worked for a company that merged with another, and when we started looking at what the new company had in inventory, we discovered that they had over 500 learner guides that had been stored in a room for two years—a retail value of about $200,000! What a waste of money. If you can negotiate the lowest possible purchase to give you flexibility, do it.

There is resistance to doing a pilot for a new program. When a program is new or just reworked, always insist on running a pilot program first, with real employees, to get a feel for how it works and to adjust details after the first run. There are always modifications that make it better; if a consultant balks at this, be cautious. Even then it might play differently with your group.

You do not have competitive market pricing. When the cost seems high to you, you either don't have a good grasp on what the service or product should cost, or it is high because you have compared it to two or three other quotes from other vendors. You need the market pricing data, or you can get burned. I always recommend that you get market pricing. This gives you a much better angle on what is going on.

You're being offered untested or new products and services. Be careful about letting your group be the "experimental group," as this presents many problems. When you are considering the purchase of a program from an outside vendor, find out how long the program has been in existence and get names and referrals. Then check them. If it is an inside resource or program, find out the same information.

The trainer is not doing a final evaluation at the end of the course. Some external and internal trainers and facilitators don't hand out critique or feedback forms for participants to complete at the end of a class. The excuse you will hear is "Well, it is just a smile sheet anyway—it's not important." Wrong! Smile sheets are the first line of information that needs to be collected after a training program. No self-respecting training professional skips this step; they want to get a feel for what participants thought of the content and the facilitator. Feedback forms should ask for both qualitative and quantitative data: written comments and ratings to questions about the course using a scale of 1 to 5 or 1 to 7. (A sample evaluation form follows this section.)

Chapter Five: Sources for Training Delivery

There is no planned follow-up. Ask a trainer or facilitator what the plans are for follow-up. Are there going to be some conference calls? E-learning? A short brush-up session? Meetings with the managers to review the information? These all need to be considered. Training really pays off when people are held accountable for using it. Insist on it.

It's an event instead of a process. Make sure that the training is not just an event, but part of a process. A process has many parts that all weave together; an event is just the event itself.

The facilitators are unskilled or inexperienced. Try not to have a facilitator who possesses a great deal of technical competence but is not a great facilitator. I have seen many people from IT or HR teach classes who knew the information better than anyone, but really struggled with public speaking and handling the dynamics of training. Okay content can be saved by a skilled facilitator, but great content can be killed by a poor one. Training is like a twin-engine plane: you need strong content *and* powerful facilitation. If either one suffers, bad things will happen.

It is up to you to determine which resources are best for your organization, and it is your decision as to whether you will use either internal or external resources. Base your decision on knowledge, resources, and research. If you do that, you will find the training that works out best for you and your team.

The Manager's Pocket Guide to Training

Evaluation and Feedback Form (Sample)

Your name: _____ Organization: _____

Phone: _____ E-mail: _____

Please circle the number that best reflects your views about the training you received. (5 = Excellent and 1 = Poor)

1. How valuable were the ideas, concepts, and program content?

    1   2   3   4   5

2. How effective was the instructor's presentation of the material?

    1   2   3   4   5

3. How would you rate the program overall?

    1   2   3   4   5

4. What are the chances that you will implement a few ideas we discussed?

    1   2   3   4   5

5. Please comment on how this seminar was helpful to you. Be as specific as you can.

    _____
    _____
    _____
    _____

6. What specific things might be done to improve this seminar in the future?

    _____
    _____
    _____
    _____

7. Other comments:

    _____
    _____
    _____

Chapter Six
Working with the Team

All leaders wonder whether or not they will know when their team needs training, and if so, what kind of training. It does take an objective eye and some analytical skills to make those determinations.

One of the best things that a leader can do alone or with other leaders is to create a SWOT analysis: an assessment of strengths, weaknesses, opportunities, and threats. When you identify the team's strengths and weaknesses, it is easier to make the right decisions about training and development. A SWOT analysis asks these questions:

SWOT Analysis

Strengths:
What are the specific strengths of your team in terms of demonstrable skills? (What they can do)
What are the strengths of your team in terms of knowledge? (What they know)
What are the strengths of the team in terms of culture and behavior?

Weaknesses:
What are the specific weaknesses of your team in terms of demonstrable skills? (What they can't do or need to do better)
What are the weaknesses of your team in terms of knowledge? (What they don't know or could know better)
What are the weaknesses of the team in terms of culture and behavior? (What could or should they change?)

Opportunities:
What are the opportunities for your team this year in terms of operational gains?
What are the opportunities this year in terms of increased efficiency?
What are the opportunities this year in terms of overall growth for the team?

Threats:
What are the threats for your team this year in terms of operational gains?
What are the threats this year in terms of increased efficiency?
What are the threats this year in terms of overall growth for the team?

The SWOT analysis provides the information you need to make some decisions about training for the coming year. Look at what kind of training the entire team needs before deciding what kind of training and development each individual member of the team needs (and each person on your team deserves development). It is best to set aside a *minimum* of one hour every year for each member of the team to discuss the individual's areas of strength and areas that need improvement. Not to be confused with the annual review, this "growth and development" meeting is a *dialogue* where only four things are discussed:

1. Strengths from the employee's view and the manager's view
2. Areas to improve from the employee's view and the manager's view
3. Career goals (short, mid, and long term)
4. Ways to achieve these goals

There are several advantages to holding such a discussion:

- It is motivating. The employee gets to talk about their favorite subject—themselves!
- If the manager handles it well, it can result in very meaningful dialogue.
- It encourages the employee to step back and think about their career.
- It builds a "track" for the manager and the employee to run on for the year.

The manager should ask the employee to fill out a self-assessment that will provide a structure for their discussion and help both parties focus on the employee's future contributions to the company. Here is what such an assessment should contain.

Chapter Six: Working with the Team

Self-Assessment for a Growth and Development Meeting

Name: _____ Date: _____

Department: _____

Strengths
What do you consider to be your top 5 skills?

What are your top 4 personal attributes (e.g., enthusiasm)?

How would you describe your overall attitude toward the job and company right now? Why?

Areas for Improvement
What three areas would you like to work on improving, and why?

What are your career goals?
1. The position I aspire to next is _____.
2. The work I want to do is _____.

Short-term career goals (the next 1–2 years):

Mid-term career goals (the next 2–3 years):

Long-term goals (3–5 years):

Individual Growth/Development Plan
What do you need to know to reach the short-term goal?

How can you gain this knowledge?

What skills need to be developed?

How can the skills be developed?

Action Plan

Describe what you plan to do, in concrete terms, to acquire the knowledge and develop the skills you will need to reach your short-term goal.

The Growth and Development Meeting

The growth and development meeting a manager has with every individual employee is the most important meeting of the year having to do with employee development, so he or she must give the meeting their full and undivided attention. The meeting should be private and not be interrupted for any reason. The manager must not multitask, be late, or cut it short out of respect for the employee. If the work environment makes a highly focused, uninterrupted meeting impossible, then the manager should schedule the meeting off-site. After all, the meeting is a commitment to the employee's development; the logistics should indicate the importance of the commitment. The manager should set the stage for the meeting by helping the employee understand the purpose of the meeting and providing them with any information ahead of time that will make the meeting as productive as possible.

Here is an example of what I mean: *"Well, Jim, I am glad we could meet today. This is the most important meeting you and I will have because it is about your development. The purpose is to talk about your strengths, areas for improvement, and your short-, mid-, and long-term goals. Then we will discuss what we can do to help get you there. I want to make sure that we have plenty of open and honest dialogue, so please feel free anytime to tell me your thoughts."*

The manager will then go through all the elements of the meeting, starting with the strengths from the self-assessment.

Their strengths. Ask the employee to review the strengths they listed on their self-assessment. This sets the stage psychologically, because the information is coming from the employee. It also gives the manager a chance to get the employee's perception of his or her strengths first. The manager should then discuss what he or she thinks the strengths are. The idea is to have

Chapter Six: Working with the Team

a substantive dialogue with plenty of specific examples. Once both parties reach mutual agreement on the strengths, the next topic can be covered.

Areas for improvement. The discussion then turns to areas for improvement. The same process is followed. Since this is a constructive discussion, the manager should avoid being critical and set a positive tone for increased understanding and dialogue.

Career goals. The employee should talk about their career goals. In the ideal world, every employee knows what they want, but in reality, many employees don't. If that is the case, the manager should try to get the employee to start to think about what they want. Do not under any circumstances try to steer the employee toward any conclusion! (If, say, a manager thinks that an employee would be great for management and the employee indicates an intense desire *not* to be in management, it would be counterproductive to try to influence that employee in that direction.)

The manager should ask the employee to talk about their mid- and long-term goals, without jumping in or prompting. The manager needs to really listen and take notes; this tells the employee that what he or she says is important to the manager. It is then time to move to the all-important individual growth and development plan.

The growth and development plan. This is the most important part of the meeting: The employee and his or her manager jointly determine specifically what the employee can do to build knowledge and skills. (Managers get better buy-in from the employee when they are involved in developing the plan.) The plan should be specific and measurable, and should include a timeline. If the growth plan seems too complex to develop at this meeting, a subsequent meeting should be scheduled. This gives the manager time to gather any resources the employee might need from the

Training and HR departments. (Think beyond the standard classroom training.) A list of resource ideas, many available at little cost, follows.

Development Resources and Opportunities	
Internal Training department	Design/Teach training class on topic
Human Resources department	Meet with company executive
External training company	Identify company subject matter expert
Off-site seminar	Vendors' and suppliers' training department
E-learning course	
Reading a book and discussion	Community college class
Internal mentor	University course
Internal coach	Joining a professional organization (e.g., Toastmasters)
External coach	
Assessment tools	Community service activity
Working at another location	Becoming a mentor
Job shadowing	Internet resources
Internet research	Brainstorm with group
Special project	Coaching from manager
Case study	Webinars
Team project	Conference calls
Other internal resources	Magazines and journals
New job function	Training videos
Coaching from a vendor	Training audio CDs
Preparation of a report on a designated topic	DVDs
	Participation in a trade organization or trade fair
Work in other departments	

Once you have an idea as to what is needed, you will need to decide what resources are needed to accomplish the team and individual training. Create a training planner like the one on the next page to think through some planning details.

Chapter Six: Working with the Team

Training Planner

What training is needed for the team?

Topic	Resources	Target Date	Estimated Costs

What training is needed for individuals?

Topic	Resources	Target Date	Estimated Costs
Name of employee #1:			
Name of employee #2:			
Name of employee #3:			
Name of employee #4:			
Name of employee #5:			
Name of employee #6:			

The Manager's Pocket Guide to Training

Now you are all set to create a budget for the development plan. Most importantly, you now have a specific strategy for training for the next year, as well as the information and data behind it to present to your manager.

Chapter Seven
Looking at the Future

Employee development by definition focuses on the future. In the previous chapter, we examined how employees and managers can lay out a strategy to prepare the employee for future roles. The manager must also be future-focused when it comes to the company. There are several elements that the leader must look at and evaluate on a continual basis.

Return on Investment

The biggest challenge of all when it comes to training is making sure that the company's investment in training is well spent. How will you truly know that training is paying off and giving you a return? As you might imagine, there are thousands of books and research papers written on the subject of training ROI and reams of research that are still producing debate. How do we measure the ROI of, say, leadership training? Is it measured by counting the number of people who move up to better positions? Is it based on their overall effectiveness as leaders after the training? And how would you measure that? So many factors affect the outcome of training that it is hard to know which ones made it more effective (or less). Was the training successful (or not successful) because of an environmental factor, such as new management or a merger? (There are Ph.D.s struggling with this question as you read this.)

Here are some simple ways to analyze your ROI:

- What kind of positive feedback have you received (on evaluation forms)?
- What kind of positive verbal feedback have you received from participants regarding the training?
- What kind of positive feedback has come in from participants' managers?
- Are you seeing differences in the team in terms of results, knowledge, and skill?
- Is turnover lower?
- Is morale better?

If you're getting positive responses from these questions, you are probably moving in the right direction.

Managing the Training Function

If you are doing all the training yourself, there is not much training management involved. However, when you have trainers or facilitators inside and outside the organization, someone has to manage the training function the same way other functions are managed. It might be more productive to hire someone to run that function and report back to you so that you can concentrate on other aspects of the operation. In either case, it is critical to have the following in place:

- A list of the organization's defined needs
- A strategy for all training (short, mid, and long term)
- A strategy for training personnel, hiring, and retention
- An infrastructure for administrative support (if needed)
- Regular contact with key users of ongoing training and stakeholders

- A strategy for vendor partnerships
- A budget for the year
- Regular reporting and communication of progress

No matter what management level you are at, it is essential that you report back to management on a regular basis and keep communicating the value of training being done and the progress being made.

Keeping up with the Training Industry

It might or might not be your responsibility to do the training or manage the training function, but clearly someone in the organization has to keep up with the latest developments in the field. There are many ways to do this.

Trade shows. Several major training conventions and shows are held around the country each year. Most include expos and seminars by industry experts.

Magazines. Most of the training associations publish their own magazines that cover trends in the industry.

Vendors. Vendors often offer clients and prospective clients white papers and other information about the field and the array of products available for purchase.

Local chapter meetings. Most of the training organizations have local chapters that meet monthly.

The training you make available to your employees can have a huge impact on you, your team, and your company. Your general knowledge and expertise on the topic will make a huge difference in your career and the results you get as a leader. Lead the way!

About the Author

Shawn Doyle, RCC, CTM

Shawn Doyle is a learning and development professional who has a passion for human development, and believes in the concept of lifelong learning. For the last 17 years, Shawn has spent his time developing and implementing training programs on sales, communication and leadership in order to help people become more effective in the workplace and in their lives. Shawn is the founder and President of New Light Learning and Development Inc., a leadership development, motivation and sales training company.

From 2000–2003 Shawn co-founded a highly successful Corporate University for a Fortune One Hundred company. In the role of Vice President of Learning and Development—he developed comprehensive leadership programs for the supervisory, managerial and executive levels. He also oversaw the development of a broad based curriculum nationwide on various topics.

From 1998–2000, he started the training function for a large advertising sales division of a major corporation. He developed highly successful sales training, leadership and mentoring programs. For his efforts in that role he won the coveted Pinnacle Award for outstanding leadership.

Shawn is certified by DDI, The Winninger Institute, Miller-Hieman, and is a Registered Corporate Coach. (RCC) he has also earned the distinction of CTM (competent Toastmaster) from Toastmasters.

Shawn is a member of the World Association of Business Coaches (WABC) The American Society of Training and Development (ASTD) and Toastmasters International.

He has had articles published in *Training and Development* magazine, *Creative Training Techniques* and Miller Heiman's *Best Few*. He is the author of *The Ten Foundations of Motivation* (iUniverse—2003) and *The Manager's Pocket Guide to Employee Motivation*

To contact Shawn for training, keynotes and consulting:

>Shawn Doyle
>President
>New Light Learning and Development
>1280 West Kings Highway
>Coatesville, Pa. 19320
>610-857-4742
>www.sldoyle.com

Made in the USA
Columbia, SC
16 December 2018